D1446866

PRESIDENTS

MILLARD
FILLMORE

A MyReportLinks.com Book

James M. Deem

MyReportLinks.com Books

an imprint of

 Enslow Publishers, Inc. **E**

Box 398, 40 Industrial Road
Berkeley Heights, NJ 07922
USA

MyReportLinks.com Books, an imprint of Enslow Publishers, Inc. MyReportLinks is a trademark of Enslow Publishers, Inc.

Library of Congress Cataloging-in-Publication Data

Deem, James M.
   Millard Fillmore / James Deem.
     p. cm. — (Presidents)
Summary: A biography of the thirteenth president of the United States, including his accomplishment of the Compromise of 1850, which helped delay the Civil War by ten years. Includes Internet links to Web sites, source documents, and photographs related to Millard Fillmore.
Includes bibliographical references (p.) and index.
   ISBN 0-7660-5074-2
   1. Fillmore, Millard, 1800–1874—Juvenile literature. 2. Presidents—United States—Biography—Juvenile literature. [1. Fillmore, Millard, 1800–1874. 2. Presidents.] I. Title. II. Series.
   E427 .D44 2003
   973.925'092—dc21

                         2002003422

Printed in the United States of America

10 9 8 7 6 5 4 3 2 1

To Our Readers:
Through the purchase of this book, you and your library gain access to the Report Links that specifically back up this book.
The Publisher will provide access to the Report Links that back up this book and will keep these Report Links up to date on **www.myreportlinks.com** for three years from the book's first publication date.
We have done our best to make sure all Internet addresses in this book were active and appropriate when we went to press. However, the author and the Publisher have no control over, and assume no liability for, the material available on those Internet sites or on other Web sites they may link to.
The usage of the MyReportLinks.com Books Web site is subject to the terms and conditions stated on the Usage Policy Statement on **www.myreportlinks.com**.
In the future, a password may be required to access the Report Links that back up this book. The password is found on the bottom of page 4 of this book.
Any comments or suggestions can be sent by e-mail to comments@myreportlinks.com or to the address on the back cover.

Photo Credits: © Corel Corporation, pp. 1 (background), 3; American Memory, The Library of Congress, p. 39; Courtesy of The National First Ladies' Library, p. 42; Dover Publications, Inc., p. 1; MyReportLinks.com Books, p. 4; PBS, pp. 12, 31; The American President, p. 17; The East Aurora Historical Society, p. 21; The Library of Congress, pp. 26, 29, 35; The Smithsonian Institution, p. 33; The United States Department of the Interior, pp. 15, 41; The United States House of Representatives, p. 25; The United States Senate, p. 30; The White House, pp. 19, 36; Tulane University, p. 23.

Cover Photo: © Corel Corporation; The Library of Congress.

Contents

Report Links............................. **4**

Highlights.............................. **10**

1 Knocking at the Door, July 9, 1850..... **11**

2 A Hungry Childhood, 1800–1819 ...... **14**

3 A Self-Made Man, 1819–1848 .... **19**

4 The Unhappy Vice President,
1849–1850............................ **28**

5 The Compromise President,
1850–1853............................ **33**

6 Fillmore's Later Years,
1853–1874............................ **39**

Chapter Notes......................... **45**

Further Reading **47**

Index **48**

MyReportLinks.com Books
Great Books, Great Links, Great for Research!

MyReportLinks.com Books present the information you need to learn about your report subject. In addition, they show you where to go on the Internet for more information. The pre-evaluated Report Links that back up this book are kept up to date on **www.myreportlinks.com**. With the purchase of a MyReportLinks.com Books title, you and your library gain access to the Report Links that specifically back up that book. The Report Links save hours of research time and link to dozens—even hundreds—of Web sites, source documents, and photos related to your report topic.

Please see "To Our Readers" on the Copyright page for important information about this book, the MyReportLinks.com Books Web site, and the Report Links that back up this book.

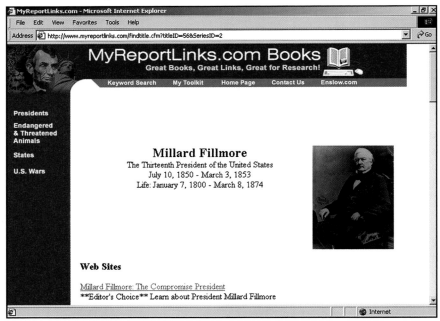

Access:

The Publisher will provide access to the Report Links that back up this book and will try to keep these Report Links up to date on our Web site for three years from the book's first publication date. Please enter **PFI1358** if asked for a password.

 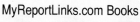

Report Links

The Internet sites described below can be accessed at
http://www.myreportlinks.com

*EDITOR'S CHOICE

▶ **Millard Fillmore: The Compromise President**
At this Web site you will find a comprehensive biography of Millard
Fillmore. Here you will learn about his early life, his life during and
after the presidency, his wife, and his impact and legacy. An image
gallery is also featured.

Link to this Internet site from http://www.myreportlinks.com

*EDITOR'S CHOICE

▶ **The American Presidency: Millard Fillmore**
This Web site offers a biography of Millard Fillmore, with facts about
his early political career, vice presidency, presidency, and later life.

Link to this Internet site from http://www.myreportlinks.com

*EDITOR'S CHOICE

▶ **Objects From the Presidency**
By navigating through this site you will find objects related to all the
United States presidents, including Millard Fillmore. You can also read
a brief description of the era he lived in and learn about the office of
the presidency.

Link to this Internet site from http://www.myreportlinks.com

*EDITOR'S CHOICE

▶ **The American President: Millard Fillmore**
This Web site contains quick facts about Millard Fillmore and his
political career. You will also learn about key events in Fillmore's
administration, find interesting trivia, and have the chance to read a
letter written by Fillmore to Congress.

Link to this Internet site from http://www.myreportlinks.com

*EDITOR'S CHOICE

▶ **The American President: "Happenstance"**
At this PBS Web site you will find an overview of Millard Fillmore's
presidency. You will also find a video clip and a quotation.

Link to this Internet site from http://www.myreportlinks.com

*EDITOR'S CHOICE

▶ **Abigail Powers Fillmore**
The official White House Web site holds the biography of First Lady
Abigail Powers Fillmore. Here you will learn about her time in the
White House, her hobbies, and her teaching career.

Link to this Internet site from http://www.myreportlinks.com

Report Links

 The Internet sites described below can be accessed at
http://www.myreportlinks.com

▶ **The Clayton-Bulwer Treaty**

At this Web site you will find the complete text of the Clayton-Bulwer Treaty. This treaty established that neither the United States nor Great Britain could have complete ownership of a canal connecting the Atlantic and Pacific Oceans.

Link to this Internet site from http://www.myreportlinks.com

▶ **Committee on Ways and Means, Millard Fillmore**

Here you will find a short article about Fillmore's role as the Chairman of the House of Representatives Ways and Means Committee from 1841 to 1843. By clicking on his photograph, you can also read a short political biography of Fillmore.

Link to this Internet site from http://www.myreportlinks.com

▶ **The Millard Fillmore House**

Take a virtual tour of the Millard Fillmore House, a National Historic Landmark, in East Aurora, New York. Fillmore built the house in the early 1820s. Included are links to related sites about Fillmore.

Link to this Internet site from http://www.myreportlinks.com

▶ **The Compromise of 1850 and the Fugitive Slave Act**

Here you will find an explanation of the Compromise of 1850. Henry Clay proposed the legislation, signed by President Fillmore, which attempted to preserve the Union.

Link to this Internet site from http://www.myreportlinks.com

▶ **Eric Foner on the Fugitive Slave Act**

At this PBS Web site, a noted historian discusses the Fugitive Slave Act, the most controversial piece of legislation passed during President Fillmore's term.

Link to this Internet site from http://www.myreportlinks.com

▶ **Fillmore, Millard**

This site features a brief profile of Millard Fillmore's administration. You will also find links to pertinent documents and a portion of Fillmore's first annual message to Congress.

Link to this Internet site from http://www.myreportlinks.com

Report Links

 The Internet sites described below can be accessed at
http://www.myreportlinks.com

▶**Fugitive Slave Act**

At this Web site you will find a brief introduction to the Fugitive Slave Act and the full text of the act signed into law by Millard Fillmore.

Link to this Internet site from http://www.myreportlinks.com

▶**Know-Nothing Party**

This Web site provides a history of the Know-Nothing Party, whose presidential candidate in 1856 was Millard Fillmore.

Link to this Internet site from http://www.myreportlinks.com

▶**Library of Congress: Millard Fillmore**

This site, from the Library of Congress, features three portraits of Millard Fillmore.

Link to this Internet site from http://www.myreportlinks.com

▶**Millard Fillmore**

The official White House Web site holds the biography of President Millard Fillmore. Here you will learn about his presidency and the Compromise of 1850.

Link to this Internet site from http://www.myreportlinks.com

▶**Millard Fillmore**

Factmonster provides a brief introduction to Millard Fillmore. Here you will learn about his life and presidency.

Link to this Internet site from http://www.myreportlinks.com

▶**Millard Fillmore**

At this Web site you will find essential information about Millard Fillmore including facts about his early life, political career, and later years.

Link to this Internet site from http://www.myreportlinks.com

Report Links

 The Internet sites described below can be accessed at
http://www.myreportlinks.com

▶ **Millard Fillmore**
At this Web site you will find facts and figures about Millard Fillmore including the offices he held during his political career, election results, and lists of his cabinet members.

Link to this Internet site from http://www.myreportlinks.com

▶ **Millard Fillmore's Obituary**
Fillmore's obituary, as it appeared in the *New York Times* on March 9, 1874, is presented. Here you can learn how the president was perceived in his own time.

Link to this Internet site from http://www.myreportlinks.com

▶ **Millard Fillmore (1800–1874)**
At the National Portrait Gallery Web site you can view a portrait of Millard Fillmore. You will also find a brief biography of the thirteenth president.

Link to this Internet site from http://www.myreportlinks.com

▶ **Mr. President: Millard Fillmore**
At this Web site you will find a short profile of Millard Fillmore, a quote, and fast facts about his life.

Link to this Internet site from http://www.myreportlinks.com

▶ **President Fillmore's Letter to the Emperor of Japan**
At this Web site you can read the letter that President Fillmore sent to the emperor of Japan. The letter helped to open up trade between the United States and Japan.

Link to this Internet site from http://www.myreportlinks.com

▶ **President Millard Fillmore**
An overview of the life of Millard Fillmore is offered as well as an interesting fact about him, a list of his cabinet members, and list of the key events of his short administration.

Link to this Internet site from http://www.myreportlinks.com

Report Links

 The Internet sites described below can be accessed at
http://www.myreportlinks.com

▶**President Millard Fillmore**
At this Web site you will find a brief biography of Millard Fillmore,
who became president upon Zachary Taylor's death. You will also find a
brief biography of other United States presidents.

Link to this Internet site from http://www.myreportlinks.com

▶**Table of Contents — The Life and Public Services of
Millard Fillmore**
This site, from the Abraham Lincoln Historical Digitization project,
offers the complete text of W. L. Barre's 1856 biography of President
Millard Fillmore.

Link to this Internet site from http://www.myreportlinks.com

▶**Thurlow Weed**
This Tulane University Web page provides a biography of Thurlow
Weed. A newspaper publisher and influential Whig politician, Weed
helped Fillmore early in his career and then worked to undermine his
stature as vice president and, later, president.

Link to this Internet site from http://www.myreportlinks.com

▶**Vice Presidents of the United States: Millard Fillmore
(1849–1850)**
This article, from the United States Senate Web site, provides a
biography of Millard Fillmore with an emphasis on his vice presidency.
You will also find many helpful bibliographical resources.

Link to this Internet site from http://www.myreportlinks.com

▶**The White House Historical Association**
By navigating through this site you can find information on Millard
Fillmore's time in the White House. You can also take a virtual tour of
the White House.

Link to this Internet site from http://www.myreportlinks.com

▶**Zachary Taylor**
At this Web site you will find a comprehensive biography of Zachary
Taylor, the twelfth U.S. president, whose death ushered Vice President
Millard Fillmore into the highest office in the land.

Link to this Internet site from http://www.myreportlinks.com

Highlights

1800—*Jan. 7:* Born in Locke, New York.

1819–1823—Studies law.

1823–1830—Practices law in East Aurora, New York.

1826—*Feb. 5:* Marries Abigail Powers.

1828—Elected to New York State Assembly.

—*April 25:* Son, Millard Powers, born.

1832—Opens law office in Buffalo, New York. Elected to United States House of Representatives.

—*March 27:* Daughter, Mary Abigail, born.

1847—Elected comptroller of New York.

1848—Nominated for vice president at the Whig National Convention in Philadelphia; elected vice-president of the United States.

1850—Upon Zachary Taylor's death, becomes thirteenth president of the United States. Signs Fugitive Slave Law.

1853—Sends Commodore Matthew Perry to open trade with Japan. Defeated in bid for presidential nomination.

1853—*March 30:* Wife, Abigail Fillmore, dies in Washington, D.C.

1854—*July 26:* Daughter Mary Abigail dies.

1856—Nominated for president of the United States by the Know-Nothing Party and the Whigs; defeated in the election.

1858—*Feb. 10:* Marries Caroline C. McIntosh.

1862—Founds and becomes first president of the Buffalo Historical Society.

1874—*March 8:* Dies in Buffalo, New York.

Chapter 1 ▶

Knocking at the Door, July 9, 1850

The knocking at the door on the night of July 9, 1850, did not surprise Vice President Millard Fillmore. He had been expecting it.

Seated alone in his room at the Willard Hotel in Washington, D.C., Fillmore had spent part of the evening trying to answer letters. But his mind was preoccupied with what was happening elsewhere in the nation's capital. He would have passed the time with his wife, but she had left town a month earlier to escape the heat and humidity of the Washington summer. So he waited alone for the messenger.

When Fillmore opened the door, a breathless man handed him a note written by members of President Zachary Taylor's cabinet: "Sir: The . . . painful duty devolves on us to announce to you that Zachary Taylor . . . is no more. . . ."[1]

Taylor, the twelfth president of the United States, had died after a brief and sudden illness. The next day, Millard Fillmore became the thirteenth president of the United States.

Only five days earlier, on the Fourth of July, President Taylor had been well. But cholera, an infectious disease, was sweeping the nation. Doctors had warned everyone against drinking milk and eating raw fruits and vegetables during the epidemic. Taylor stubbornly drank iced milk and ate fresh cherries.

On July 9, President Taylor became gravely ill. Vice President Fillmore and members of the cabinet waited

near the president's bedroom. Fillmore had been told to expect the worst. He returned to the hotel.

At 10:35 that night, President Taylor died. A messenger delivered the awful news to Vice President Fillmore who sent a short reply to the cabinet: "I have no language to express the emotions of my heart. The shock is so sudden and unexpected that I am overwhelmed with grief. . . . I . . . shall appoint a time and place for taking the oath of office. . . ."[2] Fillmore could not sleep that night. He was in one of the most difficult situations of his life: Not only had

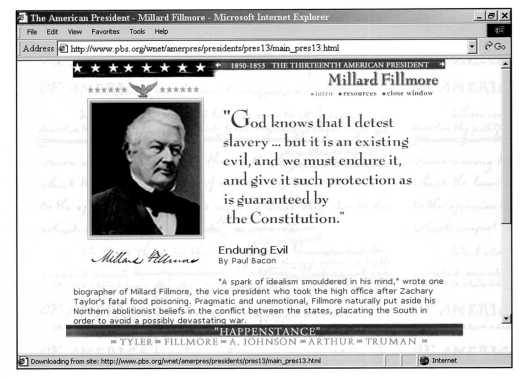

After becoming president, Millard Fillmore was faced with a grave dilemma: Abolish slavery in new territories and states, or keep the Union intact. Although he was personally opposed to slavery, Fillmore made a difficult choice that he hoped would keep the nation together.

he suddenly and unexpectedly become the president of the United States under terrible circumstances, but the nation was facing a great crisis—the awful possibility of a civil war. The Northern and Southern states were divided over the question of slavery. It was the responsibility of the president to handle the situation. Fillmore faced an enormous problem: He could either lead the country to a peaceful resolution or bring about a civil war.

That sleepless night, Fillmore thought about his life and his beliefs and the battles he would face as president. In describing the experience, he later wrote that he reviewed in his mind his own opposition to slavery. But he was aware that he could not solve the nation's debate over slavery with a simple answer—or by choosing sides.

Instead, he concluded that he must work for the good of the *entire* country, not just one region of it. By doing this, he realized that he would lose ". . . the friendship of many men . . . especially in my own state, and encounter their reproaches." But, he reasoned, ". . . to me, this is nothing. The man who can look upon a crisis without being willing to offer himself upon the altar of his country is not fit for public trust."[3]

Chapter 2

A Hungry Childhood, 1800–1819

Millard Fillmore was born in a small log cabin on a remote farm in western New York on January 7, 1800. The second of nine children, he had five brothers and three sisters. His father and grandfather were both named Nathaniel. His grandfather had fought in the Revolutionary War. His mother was Phoebe Millard, for whom Millard was named. His family was poor and lived on a farm that they had leased. Millard's cradle was a wooden trough that had been used to collect maple-sugar sap.[1]

From an early age, Millard helped his father work the farm. He learned to clear and plow the land, and he tended the meager crops. The work was backbreaking. Although he did his chores willingly, Millard looked for fun as well, something that did not please his father. When he tried to enjoy himself by hunting, fishing, or swimming, his father would warn Millard, "No man ever prospered from wasting his time in sporting."[2] Despite his father's reproaches, Millard managed to swim and fish often.

Millard's education was limited. The farm required a great deal of work, and he could attend school only in the winter months. "Consequently," he later wrote, "I forgot nearly as much during the summer as I learned in the winter."[3] Although he learned to be a good speller, he had no dictionary to look up the definitions of the words. He learned geography facts, but his school had no maps or atlases. In fact, Millard never saw a printed map or an atlas until he was nineteen years old.[4]

Nathaniel Fillmore believed that farming was a miserable job. He did not want Millard or any of his other sons to become farmers. Millard learned this lesson well in his childhood. He had no desire to follow in his father's footsteps.

▶ Learning a Trade

Instead, Millard tried making his own way. At fourteen, he wanted to join the army to fight in the War of 1812 against Britain. "I was anxious to try the life of a soldier and asked my father's permission to go for three months as

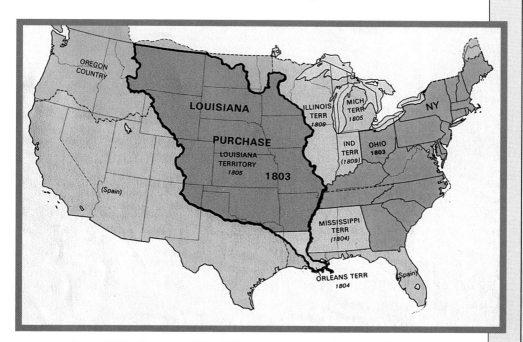

▲ In 1800, the year Millard Fillmore was born, the United States was also in its infancy—a new nation with few large cities and a great deal of wilderness. This map shows America's territorial growth by 1810, when Fillmore lived on a farm in the sparsely populated lands of western New York.

a substitute for someone who was drafted, but he refused," Millard later wrote in a letter.[5] Nathaniel Fillmore wanted his son to learn a trade, so he arranged for Millard to work for three months in a cloth-making mill. If the trial period was successful, Millard would be apprenticed for the job.

Millard walked about a hundred miles to Sparta, New York, and found the job was not to his liking. First, he disliked the meals: boiled salt pork and occasional buckwheat cakes. At home, he could eat bread and drink milk three times a day. In Sparta, milk was considered a luxury. Second, he disliked his duties. He thought he would learn a trade at the mill, but instead he spent much of his time chopping wood.

In his autobiography, Millard Fillmore described an incident that occurred one day when his boss, Benjamin Hungerford, ordered him to chop more wood. Millard became angry when he realized that he could have stayed at his family's farm to chop wood.

". . . I have submitted to this injustice long enough," Millard remembered telling Hungerford. "I will chastise you for your disobedience," Hungerford replied and threatened to strike him. "You will not chastise me," Millard told him. He was holding an axe; he raised it over his head. "If you approach me I will split you down."[6]

Hungerford walked away. The next day he asked Millard if he would like to return home, ending the trial job. Millard agreed to stay until his three months were finished. He commented:

> I am inclined to think it was unjustifiable rebellion, or at least that my threat of knocking him down was going too far, for I fear I should have executed it; and my only justification or apology is that I have an inborn hatred of injustice and tyranny which I cannot repress.[7]

Tools   Search   Notes   Discuss   Go!

This strong dislike of injustice, which would later be seen in his opposition to slavery, guided Millard throughout his life.

A Desire for Education

Millard returned home in January 1815. His father found him another apprenticeship at another cloth-making mill, this time nearer home. He was able to help his father with the farm in the spring, fulfill his apprenticeship in the summer and fall, and, most important, attend school in

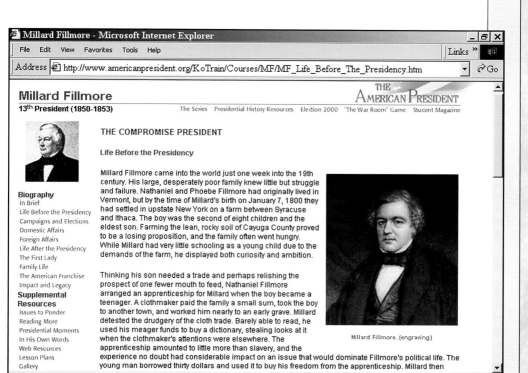

Millard Fillmore's formal education was limited, but his desire to learn was not. While helping his father on the farm and acting as an apprentice at a mill, the young Fillmore joined a library and read every book he could.

the winter. Perhaps because the Fillmores owned few books—only an almanac, a hymnbook, and a Bible—Millard joined a circulating library that became an important part of his education. He read almost any book available and soon realized how limited his vocabulary was.

Millard purchased a dictionary and took every opportunity to learn new words. He gained enough of an education to become a teacher. During the winter of 1818, he taught at a school for ten dollars a month.

At the end of the winter, Millard found another job in a sawmill where he worked for a few months. By June 1818, Millard was fulfilling the requirements of his apprenticeship. When winter came around, he thought more about getting a better education. He had heard of a good school, an academy in New Hope, New York, but it was farther from home and he would have to eat meals away. He had no money for food, so he found a farmer who lived near the school and arranged to cut wood in exchange for his meals.

As Millard Fillmore approached his nineteenth birthday, this unquenched thirst for more knowledge would take him in unexpected directions.

A Self-Made Man, 1819–1848

When Millard Fillmore was nineteen years old, he met two people who changed his life: Abigail Powers and Judge Walter Wood.

Twenty-one-year-old Abigail Powers taught at the academy in New Hope where she was impressed with her motivated new student, Millard Fillmore. He, in turn, was

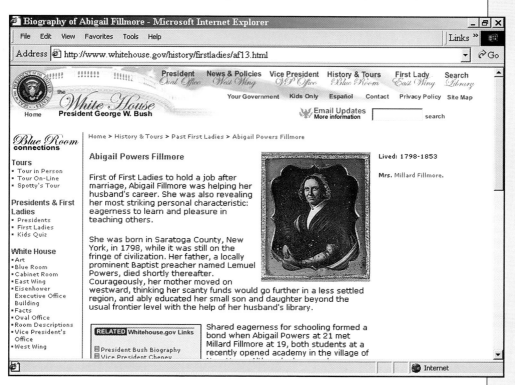

▲ Abigail Powers was Millard Fillmore's teacher at New Hope. Although they met in 1819, they were not married until 1826.

quite taken with his teacher. She was bright and pretty, and she loved to read. They shared many of the same ambitions and dreams and quickly fell in love.

Fillmore's courtship of Abigail was interrupted when Nathaniel Fillmore left his rented farm and moved his family twelve miles away. He became a tenant farmer for Judge Walter Wood, the wealthiest man in the area. Nathaniel asked Judge Wood to allow his son to clerk in his law office for two months.

Fillmore reported to Judge Wood, who handed him a book on English law and instructed him to read it. At first, Fillmore had difficulty understanding the legal writings, but he tried his best. He also traveled throughout the county on business for the judge.

▶ The Practice of Law

At the end of the two months, Judge Wood offered Fillmore the opportunity to stay. "If thee has an ambition for distinction," Fillmore remembered Judge Wood saying, "and can sacrifice everything else to success, the law is the road that leads to honors; . . . I would advise thee to come back again and study law."[1]

Fillmore, however, was obligated to continue his apprenticeship for another eighteen months. Instead, he arranged to pay his employers thirty dollars to dissolve their contract. Since he had no money, Fillmore taught school during the winter of 1820 to repay his debt. At the end of the winter, he paid his former employers and returned to work in Judge Wood's office.

By now, Fillmore was a respected teacher in his community. In a letter of recommendation for him, Fillmore was described as ". . . a capable active enterprising young

The Millard Fillmore House

A National Historic Landmark

▲ Millard Fillmore built this house in East Aurora, New York, outside Buffalo, in the early 1820s. Now a National Historic Landmark, it is open to the public.

man of strict integrity and good moral character . . . of unimpeachable standing in our society."[2]

Now a law clerk, not a farmer or mill worker, he had become known as Mr. Fillmore. Living on money borrowed from the judge, he bought respectable white collars for his shirts and added a stylish new walking stick to his attire. But Fillmore was troubled by some of Judge Wood's business practices, especially the forced eviction of some farmers. To Fillmore, the judge appeared not to care for the welfare of his tenants.

▶ On His Own

Fillmore wanted to make his own way in the world, but this did not please Judge Wood.

When Fillmore was offered three dollars to represent a man in a simple lawsuit, he accepted. This would be his first paid case without relying on the judge.

When Judge Wood heard that Fillmore had accepted payment, he became angry. The men argued. Fillmore believed that the judge was ". . . more anxious to keep me in a state of dependence and use me as a drudge in his business than to make a lawyer of me."[3] As a result, Fillmore left Judge Wood's law firm. He told the judge he would repay him the money he had borrowed.

Fillmore returned to teaching and handled a few lawsuits. He was eager to continue his law studies, but there were no opportunities in the rural area where he lived. He moved to Buffalo, New York, a bustling city of 4,000 residents. There he taught school and took an unpaid job as a clerk in a law office during the summer. Fillmore planned once more to become a lawyer.

In less than a year, the lawyers who had hired him were so impressed with the quality of his work that they recommended he practice law. He passed an examination and was admitted to the state bar in 1823. He chose to move to East Aurora, New York, a village that had no lawyers.

▶ A New Family

For two years, Fillmore practiced law and made little money. But he became an important citizen of East Aurora. He even provided space in his law office so that the village could establish its own library.

Tools   Search   Notes   Discuss   Go!

Although he had not seen her in three years, Fillmore had not forgotten Abigail Powers. They wrote letters to each other, and when he had saved enough money, he visited her. On February 5, 1826, they were married in Moravia, New York, at the home of Abigail's brother.

The year 1828 was an important one for Fillmore. His wife gave birth to their first child, a son, on April 28. They named him Millard Powers Fillmore. Later that year, Fillmore was elected to the first of three one-year terms in the New York State Assembly. He had become an active

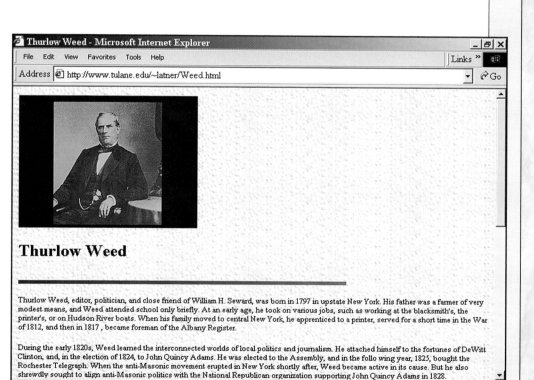

Thurlow Weed - Microsoft Internet Explorer

File   Edit   View   Favorites   Tools   Help   Links »

Address http://www.tulane.edu/~latner/Weed.html   Go

Thurlow Weed

Thurlow Weed, editor, politician, and close friend of William H. Seward, was born in 1797 in upstate New York. His father was a farmer of very modest means, and Weed attended school only briefly. At an early age, he took on various jobs, such as working at the blacksmith's, the printer's, or on Hudson River boats. When his family moved to central New York, he apprenticed to a printer, served for a short time in the War of 1812, and then in 1817, became foreman of the Albany Register.

During the early 1820s, Weed learned the interconnected worlds of local politics and journalism. He attached himself to the fortunes of DeWitt Clinton, and, in the election of 1824, to John Quincy Adams. He was elected to the Assembly, and in the following year, 1825, bought the Rochester Telegraph. When the anti-Masonic movement erupted in New York shortly after, Weed became active in its cause. But he also shrewdly sought to align anti-Masonic politics with the National Republican organization supporting John Quincy Adams in 1828.

Done   Internet

Politician and journalist Thurlow Weed became friends with Millard Fillmore when both served in the New York State Assembly. Weed later worked to undermine Fillmore during Fillmore's term as vice president.

member of the Anti-Masonic Party in New York. The Anti-Masonic Party, which started in New York in 1828, opposed the power wielded by politicians who were Freemasons, part of a secret society. Its members were opposed to Andrew Jackson and his Democratic policies.

As an Anti-Mason, Fillmore became friends with an influential newspaper editor and Anti-Masonic political leader named Thurlow Weed. Weed's friendship helped Fillmore in his early political career.

▶ In the State Assembly

On Christmas 1828, Fillmore left home to travel to Albany, the state capital, to take his seat in the state assembly. It was the first time he had been separated from his wife since their wedding. She wrote him almost every day, telling him about life at home.

During his first year, Fillmore quickly developed the skills that would enhance his reputation as a prominent legislator. A local newspaper reporter described Fillmore this way:

> Although the age of Mr. Fillmore does not exceed thirty years, he has all the prudence, discretion, and judgment of an experienced man. He is modest, retiring, and unassuming. . . . He seldom speaks, unless there appears to be an absolute necessity for the arguments or explanations which he offers. Nor does he ever rise without attracting the attention of all who are within the sound of his voice—a tribute of respect paid to his youthful modesty and great good sense.[4]

Fillmore revealed a passionate side when it came to two issues. First, he cared about people who were weak and unprotected. He submitted a bill that made it illegal to imprison a person because he was in debt. The bill passed. Second, he cared about the separation of church and state.

He introduced another bill that would have stopped religious oaths in courtroom trials. At the time, a witness who did not swear a belief in God was not permitted to testify in a New York State court. However, this bill did not pass.

By the end of his third term, Fillmore decided to retire from the assembly and return to personal life. But he did not retire from politics.

Buffalonian

In 1830, Fillmore moved his family from East Aurora to Buffalo. The Fillmores settled into an active social life,

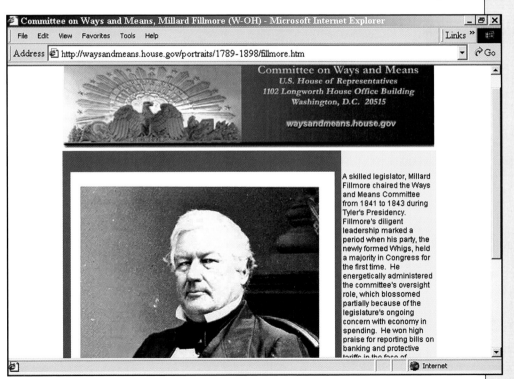

Committee on Ways and Means, Millard Fillmore (W-OH) - Microsoft Internet Explorer

File   Edit   View   Favorites   Tools   Help   Links »

Address http://waysandmeans.house.gov/portraits/1789-1898/fillmore.htm   Go

Committee on Ways and Means
U.S. House of Representatives
1102 Longworth House Office Building
Washington, D.C. 20515

waysandmeans.house.gov

A skilled legislator, Millard Fillmore chaired the Ways and Means Committee from 1841 to 1843 during Tyler's Presidency. Fillmore's diligent leadership marked a period when his party, the newly formed Whigs, held a majority in Congress for the first time. He energetically administered the committee's oversight role, which blossomed partially because of the legislature's ongoing concern with economy in spending. He won high praise for reporting bills on banking and protective tariffs in the face of

Elected to the United States House of Representatives four times, Millard Fillmore became the chairman of the Ways and Means Committee—a position of great power and responsibility.

Fillmore, who started out in politics as an Anti-Mason and later joined the Whig Party, became Zachary Taylor's running mate in the 1848 presidential campaign. This campaign banner pictures Taylor on the left and Fillmore on the right.

attending dinners, recitals, and theatrical performances. They joined the Unitarian Church. They expanded their personal library that eventually numbered 4,000 volumes.

Their daughter, Mary Abigail, was born on March 27, 1832. That same year, Fillmore opened a law office in Buffalo. He represented clients in transportation, education, and finance—institutions important to the growth and development of Buffalo. He also helped create the Buffalo Fire Department. Later that year he was elected a representative from New York to the United States Congress.

In the Nation's Capital

Fillmore was elected four times to the House of Representatives. He first served as an Anti-Mason from 1833 to 1835. He then switched parties and served as a member of the Whig Party from 1837 to 1843. The Whigs opposed President Andrew Jackson and the Democrats. Filmore was appointed chairman of the Ways and Means Committee, a powerful financial position. In 1842 he chose not to run for reelection and returned home to Buffalo.

In 1847, Fillmore was elected New York State comptroller, overseeing the state's entire budget. In many ways, the position was more powerful than that of the governor because the comptroller was responsible for shaping the economy of New York. By the time the Whig Party held its presidential convention for the election of 1848, Fillmore had achieved a national reputation. When Zachary Taylor was nominated for president, Fillmore was selected as his running mate.

Chapter 4 ▶

The Unhappy Vice President, 1849–1850

Zachary Taylor won the presidency in 1848 by a small margin, provided in part by the voters of Fillmore's home state of New York. Millard Fillmore had come a long way from his humble beginnings. He had worked and studied to provide a better life for himself and his family. Now, he had prestige as vice president of the United States.

Fillmore had the potential to be influential in Taylor's administration. In fact, President-elect Zachary Taylor expressed a desire that ". . . Mr. Fillmore would take all of the business into his own hands. . . ."[1] Taylor had little knowledge of politics and protocols. He had made a name for himself as a general in the Mexican-American War, not as a politician. He had never even voted in an election. When creating his cabinet, however, Taylor never consulted with his vice president, even though Fillmore had been a politician for almost twenty years.

Fillmore was not to have any influence in Taylor's administration. His former friend, newspaper editor Thurlow Weed, had begun to scheme behind Fillmore's back. Weed wanted his friend, William Henry Seward, to become president of the United States. Weed and Seward viewed Fillmore as a threat to this plan.

Seward wasted no time gaining the favor of President Taylor and his family. Soon Seward, rather than Fillmore, was advising the president. Millard Fillmore's advice was ignored.

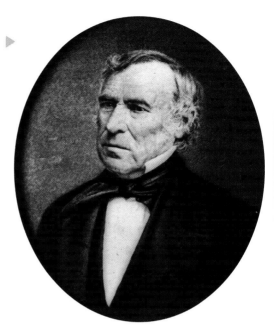

Zachary Taylor, the twelfth president of the United States, had no experience as a politician when he was elected president. But instead of seeking the advice of his vice president, Millard Fillmore, who had much more experience, he turned elsewhere for help.

Scheming for Patronage

Fillmore was overwhelmed by requests for patronage, or political appointments. Superintendents of the Erie Canal, postmasters, and money collectors were appointed to jobs, and many politicians in New York believed that Fillmore owed it to the state and to his political friends to fill positions with his allies.

Fillmore detested the idea of patronage. In a form letter that he sent to anyone inquiring for a patronage job, he wrote:

> The vice president has no patronage and is in no wise connected with the executive branch of the government. The appointing power is exclusively in the president and Senate and the heads of the several departments. . . . I would cheerfully refer any petitions or recommendations to departments and if asked for opinion as to who was most suitable would gladly give it. . . . I shall not commit myself in advance for or against any candidate.[2]

▲ As the vice president of the United States, Fillmore was the president of the Senate. This painting by Peter Rothermel shows Henry Clay (standing, center) presenting his compromise to the Senate in 1850, with Fillmore (seated at top, right) presiding.

Thurlow Weed had no such qualms. As a result, many patronage jobs in New York were given to his friends. "We could put up a cow against a Fillmore nominee and defeat him," a Weed newspaper, the *Buffalo Express*, bragged.[3]

Fillmore expressed his frustration in a letter he wrote to a friend on July 11, 1849: "I do not feel that I have any responsibility as connected with this administration. . . . My advice has neither been sought nor given as to the policy to be followed."[4]

The Compromise of 1850

The most serious problem facing the Taylor administration was the debate over the issue of slavery in the territories. At that time, there were fifteen free states and fifteen slave states. Each state had two senators and thus two electoral votes. The issue was whether a territory soon to become a state, such as California, should enter the Union as a free state. If so, that would upset the balance of power. There was increasing tension between the North, which opposed

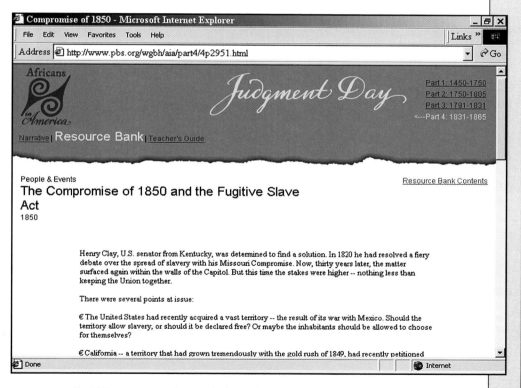

Compromise of 1850 - Microsoft Internet Explorer

File   Edit   View   Favorites   Tools   Help   Links »

Address http://www.pbs.org/wgbh/aia/part4/4p2951.html   Go

Africans in America

Judgment Day

Part 1: 1450-1750
Part 2: 1750-1805
Part 3: 1791-1831
<---Part 4: 1831-1865

Narrative | Resource Bank | Teacher's Guide

People & Events   Resource Bank Contents

The Compromise of 1850 and the Fugitive Slave Act
1850

Henry Clay, U.S. senator from Kentucky, was determined to find a solution. In 1820 he had resolved a fiery debate over the spread of slavery with his Missouri Compromise. Now, thirty years later, the matter surfaced again within the walls of the Capitol. But this time the stakes were higher -- nothing less than keeping the Union together.

There were several points at issue:

€ The United States had recently acquired a vast territory -- the result of its war with Mexico. Should the territory allow slavery, or should it be declared free? Or maybe the inhabitants should be allowed to choose for themselves?

€ California -- a territory that had grown tremendously with the gold rush of 1849, had recently petitioned

Done   Internet

This attempt to keep a balance between slave states and free states after the United States had acquired territory from Mexico was proposed by Senator Henry Clay in 1850. Zachary Taylor opposed the compromise, but Millard Fillmore saw it as a means to preserve the Union.

slavery in the new territories, and the South, which wanted to permit it.

Senator Henry Clay proposed a plan to keep the balance. It eventually became known as the Compromise of 1850 and consisted of five resolutions that gave something to both free and slave states. One key proposal allowed "open territories" where slavery could still be an option. President Taylor strongly opposed this plan. He believed that territories should be admitted as free states. His belief, however, angered some senators from slaveholding states. They suggested that Southern states might secede from the Union if Taylor vetoed the Compromise.

Fillmore himself was against slavery, but he was also opposed to a civil war. He believed it was in the best interest of the nation to preserve the Union, not engage in civil war. He believed that the states, not the federal government, should have the authority to permit or forbid slavery. He also believed that the Compromise of 1850 was necessary and knew that as president of the Senate he would have to break any tie with a vote in favor of the compromise. It was a difficult position.

What he did not know was that Taylor would die unexpectedly on July 9, 1850. Fillmore would be left to confront this issue as president.

Chapter 5 ▶

The Compromise President, 1850–1853

Millard Fillmore became the thirteenth president of the United States without fanfare and without the presence of his family. At noon on July 10, 1850, he was given the oath of office before a joint session of Congress. That same night, each member of President Taylor's cabinet

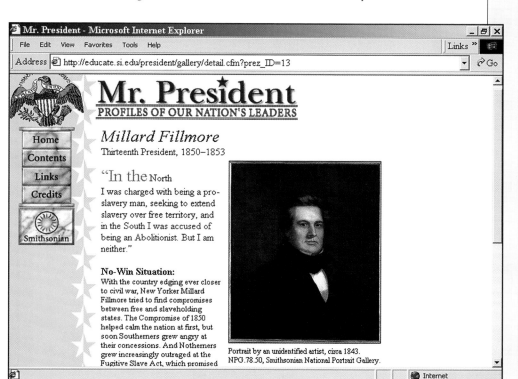

Mr. President - Microsoft Internet Explorer

File   Edit   View   Favorites   Tools   Help   Links »

Address http://educate.si.edu/president/gallery/detail.cfm?prez_ID=13   Go

Mr. President
PROFILES OF OUR NATION'S LEADERS

Home
Contents
Links
Credits
Smithsonian

Millard Fillmore
Thirteenth President, 1850–1853

"In the North I was charged with being a pro-slavery man, seeking to extend slavery over free territory, and in the South I was accused of being an Abolitionist. But I am neither."

No-Win Situation:
With the country edging ever closer to civil war, New Yorker Millard Fillmore tried to find compromises between free and slaveholding states. The Compromise of 1850 helped calm the nation at first, but soon Southerners grew angry at their concessions. And Northerners grew increasingly outraged at the Fugitive Slave Act, which promised

Portrait by an unidentified artist, circa 1843.
NPG.78.50, Smithsonian National Portrait Gallery.

▲ After Zachary Taylor died in office, Vice President Millard Fillmore was thrust into the presidency at a time when Southern states were threatening to secede from the Union. The decisions that Fillmore had to make in his short tenure as president were difficult ones.

offered a letter of resignation. They agreed to remain only one more week, which forced Fillmore to find an acceptable cabinet quickly.

Now that Fillmore was president, he had the power and the opportunity to change any or all of Taylor's patronage appointments. Instead, Fillmore replaced only one appointee: the collector of the Port of Buffalo. He had more pressing matters at hand than personal revenge.

▶ Compromising on Slavery

The Compromise of 1850 that had divided Congress still faced a vote. Fillmore realized that it would be impossible to include the five proposals in one bill and have it passed. He encouraged Senator Stephen A. Douglas to break the compromise into five separate bills, each acceptable to a different majority and to different parts of the nation. As Congress passed each bill, Fillmore signed it into law.

As a result, California was admitted to the Union as a free state; the selling of slaves became illegal in the District of Columbia (although slavery itself was not banned there); New Mexico and Utah became territories that could decide for themselves whether to adopt slavery; and Texas surrendered 40 percent of its territory to New Mexico.

However, one of the bills, the Fugitive Slave Act, troubled Fillmore. The law gave the federal government authority over slaves who had run away. If a slave escaped to a free state, the Fugitive Slave Act required federal authorities to return the slave to his or her master without the benefit of a jury trial.

Southern slaveholders applauded the new law, but Northern abolitionists (people opposed to slavery) refused to obey it. Fillmore's wife, Abigail, advised her husband not to sign the bill, but he felt obligated to sign into law any bill that Congress passed. Fillmore reluctantly signed the law and received many death threats as a result.

> I have been frequently threatened with assassination by anonymous letters from the North, from the South. . . . I can assure you that such threats will never deter me from the performance of my duty. I know I must die, and I choose to meet my fate in the discharge of my duty.[1]

This photograph of Millard Fillmore was taken by Mathew Brady, who would later become famous for his Civil War photographs.

Although the Compromise of 1850 did not solve the issue of slavery, it stalled the onset of the Civil War for almost ten years.

▶ A Vision for Commerce

Fillmore believed that business would produce a prosperous America. He supported the idea of the transcontinental railroad and arranged federal land grants to aid in the development of railroads. In Central America, he supported a link, whether by rail or by canal, from the Gulf of

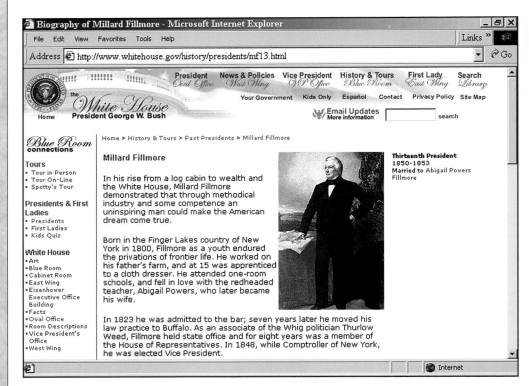

▲ Raised in a log cabin, and with little formal schooling, Millard Fillmore rose to the highest office in the land in becoming the thirteenth president of the United States.

Mexico to the Pacific Ocean. Both visions would be realized under later presidents.

At the same time, Fillmore did not support the idea of Manifest Destiny—that America had a right to claim and occupy all of North America. For example, he wanted to maintain the independence of the Hawaiian islands. Although the Hawaiian king gave Fillmore the option of annexing Hawaii, he preferred to keep Hawaii independent. Greedy entrepreneurs encouraged him to take possession of Cuba and even islands off the coast of Peru. Fillmore refused.

▶ Opening Trade With Japan

The important event in foreign policy during Fillmore's administration was the opening of Japan to trade with other nations. Japan had closed its ports to all foreigners except Dutch merchants. For more than two hundred years, the island nation had shut itself off from the rest of the world and lived in isolation.

President Fillmore knew that trade with other countries was a source of wealth for the United States. When he became president, American ships were trading around the world. Fillmore wanted to increase American trade with Asia and reopen trade with Japan. The United States also wanted port privileges in southern Japan where American vessels could refuel on their way across the Pacific Ocean.

Fillmore was diligent in his attempts to make sure he followed proper protocol. He wrote a letter to the emperor of Japan, stating that he desired friendship and trade between the two nations. He commissioned Commodore Matthew Perry to sail to Japan to deliver the letter. In July 1853 after a six-month voyage, Perry led four American warships into Tokyo Bay. He presented the letter during an

elaborate ceremony. Although the emperor did not meet personally with Perry, he received the letter.

The following spring, Perry returned with four extra warships. This new show of force convinced the emperor to sign a peace treaty and a trade agreement. Although Fillmore left office before the treaty was signed, it was a major foreign policy accomplishment for his presidency.

Chapter 6

Fillmore's Later Years, 1853–1874

The Compromise of 1850 had left President Fillmore with little desire to run for a new term as president. He did not even campaign for a nomination. Winfield Scott became his party's nominee but was defeated in the election by Democrat Franklin Pierce.

Fillmore left office on March 4, 1853. He had served

MILLARD FILLMORE,

AMERICAN CANDIDATE FOR PRESIDENT OF THE UNITED STATES.

▲ This campaign poster for the 1856 presidential election shows Fillmore as a candidate for the American Party, also known as the Know-Nothing Party.

only two years, seven months, and twenty-three days. He and Abigail had already sent their belongings back to Buffalo. But during Pierce's inauguration, Abigail sat outside in a cold, gusty wind with her feet covered in slush. By the next morning, she had become seriously ill with a cold that quickly turned to pneumonia. On March 30, Abigail Fillmore died in Washington, D.C.

Abigail's death was a great blow to Fillmore. "The light of the house is gone," he wrote to a friend, "and I can never hope to enjoy life again as I have heretofore."[1] Lonely and heartbroken, he returned to Buffalo. The following March, restless and bored, Fillmore took the trip to the South that he had planned to take with Abigail. The following year, he took a similar trip to the Midwest. He was greeted warmly everywhere he went and had many speaking engagements.

But shortly after Fillmore returned home, he faced a double tragedy: His daughter and his younger brother died unexpectedly of cholera. He wrote a friend:

> I feel life has little left for me. My good son, only of all my little family remains. . . . But I do not mean to grieve; much less complain. Heaven has blessed me many years, and has now withdrawn these precious jewels from my sight and taken them home. . . .[2]

Fillmore closed his house and sailed for Europe for a thirteen-month tour. He came out of retirement in 1856 to make a run for the presidency, as a candidate for the extremist American Party, also called the Know-Nothing Party. The party got that name because its members were urged to say they "knew nothing" about the party's secretive ways if asked. The party opposed the immigration of Catholic Irish and German immigrants. In speeches, Fillmore did not support the antiforeign sentiments of the

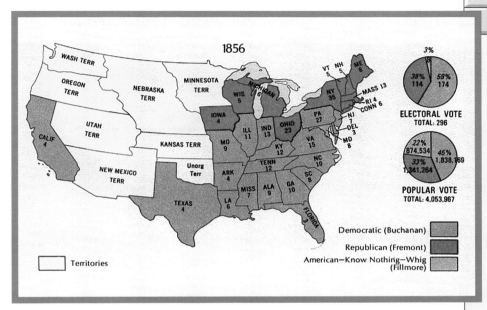

This map shows the results of the election of 1856. Fillmore, who did not even run for reelection in 1852, ran as a third-party candidate in 1856. Losing to Democrat James Buchanan, Fillmore carried only one state, Maryland, in the election.

party. "As an American, I have no hostility to foreigners. . . ." he announced. "Having witnessed their deplorable condition in the old country, God forbid I should add to their sufferings by refusing them asylum in this."[3] He lost the election to Democrat James Buchanan and managed to carry only one state, Maryland.

After that disappointing experience, Fillmore never ran for public office again. He did, however, hold prominent positions in the twenty-one years that followed his departure from the White House. He was the first chancellor of the University of Buffalo and the first president of the Buffalo Historical Society. In 1858 he married Caroline McIntosh. On February 13, 1874, he suffered a stroke.

Just two weeks later, he had another attack. On March 8, 1874, Millard Fillmore died in Buffalo, New York, at seventy-four years of age.

▶ A "Second-hand President"?

Millard Fillmore had many detractors who enjoyed criticizing him. One story that circulated shortly after his inauguration concerned a carriage. Supposedly, Fillmore was unhappy with the old carriage reserved for the president's use, and he went shopping for a replacement.

"How do you think it will do for the President of the United States to ride in a second-hand carriage?" he reportedly asked an assistant.

"Sure, you know, excellency," the assistant replied, "you're only a second-hand president."[4]

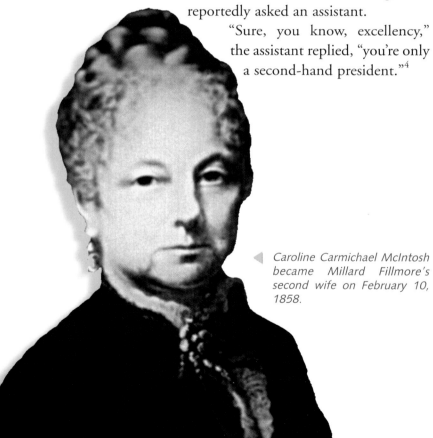

Caroline Carmichael McIntosh became Millard Fillmore's second wife on February 10, 1858.

He was also never forgiven by some people for signing the Fugitive Slave Act. In the days after Abraham Lincoln's assassination, Fillmore was targeted again. Other Buffalo residents had draped funeral cloth on their doors and windows. Fillmore's house, however, did not display any such decoration, because he was out of town at the time. Someone decided that this was a symbolic statement against Lincoln and covered his house with black ink. It is true that Fillmore was not fond of the Republican Lincoln, but Fillmore strongly supported the Union cause when the Civil War was declared, and he encouraged citizens to volunteer for the army.

▶ Final Assessment

Although Millard Fillmore wrote a great deal during his lifetime, little has been written about him since his death. In some ways, his presidency has been forgotten.

Fillmore's greatest domestic accomplishment—the passing of the Compromise of 1850—also brought about his defeat. By trying to please everyone by passing the bill in sections, he enraged a good deal of the country and essentially pleased no one.

His greatest foreign policy achievement was opening trade with Japan. That action helped the development of commerce for the United States and influenced the course of history for Japan. It led the way for Japan to change from an agricultural society to an industrial nation.

One newspaper summed him up this way: "President Fillmore is the most plain, unostentatious and simple-hearted [man] that ever governed 30,000,000 people."[5]

Fillmore himself was an example of the American dream. He pursued an education despite many hardships and attained a position of great importance. Often called

the "First Citizen of Buffalo," he was instrumental in nurturing the city's growth and commerce. As president, he made decisions that he believed were necessary. According to some historians, his actions probably postponed the Civil War by ten years. First and foremost, Millard Fillmore had wanted to save the Union.

Chapter Notes

Chapter 1. Knocking at the Door, July 9, 1850

1. Robert J. Rayback, *Millard Fillmore: Biography of a President* (Newtown, Conn.: American Political Biography Press, 1959), p. 239.

2. Robert K. Scarry, *Millard Fillmore* (Jefferson, N.C.: McFarland & Company, 2001), p. 154.

3. Rayback, p. 241.

Chapter 2. A Hungry Childhood, 1800–1819

1. Robert K. Scarry, *Millard Fillmore* (Jefferson, N.C.: McFarland & Company, 2001), p. 16.

2. Frank H. Severance, *Millard Fillmore Papers: Volume 2* (Buffalo, N.Y.: Buffalo Historical Society, 1907), p. 471.

3. Ibid., p. vii.

4. Scarry, p. 17.

5. Lockwood L. Doty, *A History of Livingstone County, New York* (Geneseo, N.Y.: 1876), p. 880.

6. Severance, pp. 6–7.

7. Doty, p. 882.

Chapter 3. A Self-Made Man, 1819–1848

1. Frank H. Severance, *Millard Fillmore Papers: Volume 1* (Buffalo, N.Y.: Buffalo Historical Society, 1907), pp. 11–13.

2. W. L. Barre, *The Life and Public Service of Millard Fillmore* (Buffalo, N.Y.: Wanzer & McKim Company, 1856), p. 50.

3. Severance, pp. 13–14.

4. Irving Chamberlain, *Biography of Millard Fillmore* (Buffalo, N.Y.: Thomas & Lathrops, 1856), pp. 41–43.

Chapter 4. The Unhappy Vice President, 1849–1850

1. Robert J. Rayback, *Millard Fillmore: Biography of a President* (Newtown, Conn.: American Political Biography Press, 1959), p. 192.

2. Robert K. Scarry, *Millard Fillmore* (Jefferson, N.C.: McFarland & Company, 2001), p. 156.

3. Rayback, p. 204.

4. Scarry, p. 167.

Chapter 5. The Compromise President, 1850–1853

1. Robert K. Scarry, *Millard Fillmore* (Jefferson, N.C.: McFarland & Company, 2001), p. 179.

Chapter 6. Fillmore's Later Years, 1853–1874

1. Robert K. Scarry, *Millard Fillmore* (Jefferson, N.C.: McFarland & Company, 2001), p. 246.

2. Ibid., p. 266.

3. Robert J. Rayback, *Millard Fillmore: Biography of a President* (Newtown, Conn.: American Political Biography Press, 1959), p. 407.

4. Scarry, p. 192.

5. Ibid., p. 238.

Further Reading

Casey, Jane Clark. *Millard Fillmore*. Chicago: Childrens Press, 1988.

Cleveland, Will, and Mark Alvarez. *Yo, Millard Fillmore (And All Those Other Presidents You Don't Know)*. Brookfield, Conn.: Millbrook Press, 1997.

Gaines, Ann Graham. *Commodore Perry Opens Japan to Trade in World History*. Berkeley Heights, N.J.: Enslow Publishers, Inc., 2000.

Graebner, Norman A. "Zachary Taylor, Millard Fillmore" in Graff, Henry F., ed., *The Presidents: A Reference History*. New York: Charles Scribner's Sons, 1984.

Joseph, Paul. *Millard Fillmore*. Edina, Minn.: ABDO Publishing, 2000.

Law, Kevin J. *Millard Fillmore: 13th President of the United States*. Ada, Okla.: Garrett Educational Corporation, 1990.

Overdyke, William Darrell. *The Know-Nothing Party in the South*. Baton Rouge: Louisiana State University Press, 1968.

Rayback, Robert J. *Millard Fillmore: Biography of a President*. Newtown, Conn.: American Political Biography Press, 1992.

Scarry, Robert K. *Millard Fillmore*. Jefferson, N.C.: McFarland & Company, 2001.

Smith, Elbert B. *The Presidencies of Zachary Taylor and Millard Fillmore*. Lawrence: University of Kansas Press, 1988.

Souter, Gerry, and Janet Souter. *Millard Fillmore: Our 13th President*. Chanhassen, Mich.: Child's World, 2001.

A

Albany, New York, 24
American Party (Know-
    Nothing Party), 40–41
Anti-Masonic Party, 24

B

Buchanan, James, 41
Buffalo, New York, 22, 25, 27,
    40, 42, 44

C

Civil War (U.S.), 13, 44
Clay, Henry, 31, 32
Compromise of 1850, 32,
    34–35, 39, 43

D

Douglas, Stephen A., 34

E

East Aurora, New York, 22, 25

F

Fillmore, Abigail Powers, (first
    wife), 19–20, 23, 34, 40
Fillmore, Caroline Carmichael
    McIntosh (second wife),
    41, 42
Fillmore, Mary Abigail
    (daughter), 27, 40
Fillmore, Millard Powers
    (son), 23
Fillmore, Nathaniel (father),
    14, 16, 17, 20
Fillmore, Phoebe Millard
    (mother), 14
Fugitive Slave Act, 34, 43

H

Hawaiian islands, 37
Hungerford, Benjamin, 16

J

Japan, 37, 43

L

Lincoln, Abraham, 43

M

Mexican-American War, 28

P

Perry, Matthew, 37–38
Pierce, Franklin, 39

S

Scott, Winfield, 39
Seward, William Henry, 28

T

Taylor, Zachary, 11–12, 27,
    28, 32

U

United States House of
    Representatives, 27

W

War of 1812, 15
Weed, Thurlow, 24, 28, 30
Whig Party, 27
Wood, Walter, 19, 20–21, 22